HÄGAR ON THE RACK

There may be some argument about which European first discovered America—an Italian or a Viking. But now the whole world has discovered that jolly Viking, Hägar the Horrible.

Hägar is back with his entire Viking crew plus Helga, Honi, Hamlet, Snert, Kvack and, of course, Lucky Eddie, Hägar's sidekick.

Here's your chance to join the more than 100 million people who "discover" and enjoy Hägar every day, in over 1600 newspapers around the world.

Hägar's creator is Dik Browne, twice winner of the Ruben Award, the National Cartoonist Society's highest honor.

Hägar the Horrible Books

HÄGAR THE HORRIBLE
HÄGAR THE HORRIBLE: ANIMAL HAUS
HÄGAR THE HORRIBLE: BORN LEADER
HÄGAR THE HORRIBLE: BRING 'EM BACK ALIVE
HÄGAR THE HORRIBLE: THE BRUTISH ARE COMING
HÄGAR THE HORRIBLE: EXCUSE ME
HÄGAR THE HORRIBLE: HAVE YOU BEEN UPTIGHT LATELY?
HÄGAR THE HORRIBLE: HÄGAR HITS THE MARK
HÄGAR THE HORRIBLE: HÄGAR'S KNIGHT OUT
HÄGAR THE HORRIBLE: HAPPY HOUR
HÄGAR THE HORRIBLE: HELGA'S REVENGE
HÄGAR THE HORRIBLE: HORNS OF PLENTY
HÄGAR THE HORRIBLE: MIDNIGHT MUNCHIES
HÄGAR THE HORRIBLE: MY FEET ARE DRUNK
HÄGAR THE HORRIBLE: NORSE CODE
HÄGAR THE HORRIBLE: ON THE LOOSE
HÄGAR THE HORRIBLE: ON THE RACK
HÄGAR THE HORRIBLE: SACK TIME
HÄGAR THE HORRIBLE: THE SIMPLE LIFE

THE HORRIBLE
ON THE RACK

BY DIK BROWNE

Ⓒ

CHARTER BOOKS, NEW YORK

HAGAR THE HORRIBLE: ON THE RACK

A Charter Book / published by arrangement with
King Features Syndicate, Inc.

PRINTING HISTORY
Tempo edition / September 1976
Charter edition / August 1986

ISBN: 0-441-31470-8

Charter Books are published by The Berkley Publishing Group,
200 Madison Avenue, New York, New York 10016.
PRINTED IN THE UNITED STATES OF AMERICA

SLAM

DIK BROWNE — 3-16

3-25

3-27

5-11